Living Mortal

~ Later Poems ~

2019 ~ 2021

Wade Dowin

First East

ISBN 9798417243080

First Published February 2, 2022

contents

The Difference Was Not

Mooses Go Walking While Universe Unmoved

Remains In Motion

The Bug

The Bird

The Bell

About the Leaves

Of Dwelling in Time

The Same As Any Star

The Hill

And So

The Friend (A Fable)

  "Today I can be grateful..."

  "This evening, looking at my hands..."

Of Seeds

  "To have reached this age..."

Now, Roses

The Fade

"It's all over now, it's all in the past"

The Curator

In Subtle Shades

  "From flash to ash..."

  "We, drawn here too..."

  "In every moment..."

Mist boats

ferrying feint hopes

to lost horizons

beneath blue moons

There is nothing new

under the sun

except for the experience

of it.

It has always been there

seen a million billion times

for the first.

All is new in every moment,
before our eyes it shimmers.
Over fifty years ago
I stood on this same hilltop
looking out over this same valley.
It would seem to me the same,
the sign says it is the same,
yet nothing remains the same.
Trees have grown or fallen
on seasons of leaves composted.
Moisture gathers, falls and flows,
carrying the valley with it grain by grain.
Insects have tilled the soil
and become parts of it.

The earth of the valley itself
has lifted or sunk
in millions of insignificant ways, compounded.
As I stand here even my own cells
are not the same that came here so long ago.
We and the world push through time and space
leaving a tailing mist of what was us.

Note to the Night

You were the one who knew
I was not always nice
I saw you never smiled
We both had friends who knew better
who ought to have said
who hid things
for the best
of intentions

We had trajectories
Poetry was in the air
Potent vapors
Things were progressing as they should
All the signs were good
as we tried to please
with good
intentions

I miss you still
or maybe it's just the time
when it was
almost

Be well

In Schultzville

All is agreed in Schultzville.
All thinking synced in Schultzville.
All confidently correct in Schultzville.
All comfortably unchallenged in Shultzville.
With certainty above all in Schultzville.
The right perceptions are reaffirmed,
The right perceptions are reaffirmed,
The right perceptions are reaffirmed,
                              in Shultzville.
There is no doubt in Schultzville.
Be assured. All is right in Schultzville.
Ya vol Herr Kommandant! in Schultzville.

Potshards

In Ten Pieces

i.

I am my own Man from Porlock

The lines would go here
but for hundreds of times lost
through all these years
Divined while mowing the lawn,
or late in the night shoveling snow
hours at a time, my Zen places

composed and recombined, in my head
erudite and enlightened,
realization and revelation,
remarkable with wry depth and perception
each word chosen precisely
infused with profundity

"I have to write this down when I'm done."

(I would resolve)

only to find, with the machine put away,

with the snow knocked off

the coats and hats shaken clean,

the lines were vanished

without a trace or a clue

Gone, leaving no shadow to be found in my skull

Not a cell holding a mark of recognition

I knew they had been there

I searched, I strained, but in vain.

Gone, just gone, I mourned for posterity

No Kubla Khan would decree

ii.

Then, and Still

"Alas, poor Yorick, I knew him...

not at all."

What jests, what lore once contained
in that most famous gourd of all?
What views flowed past those sockets?
A life of experiences once encased
become but this hollow void

He but one of the billions
with lives of sights and sounds,
joys and pains large and small, suns, stars

and moons

Mothers' comforts, in shared laughter,
or in sickness, in cold, in apprehension
all in their differing appropriations

once inhabitant, those boney abodes
tissue sparking electric
Each one a light, a name,
a word acknowledging an existence,
they blinked into being for but their moment
to leave behind these orbs and shards

On museum shelves, in dusty digs,
curiosities in dark cupboards,
pictures in books or magazines
Reminders forgotten and forgetting
they silently continue their slow crawl
atom by atom until dispersed

Or lying in graves or desert, fallen
in field or forest or bottom of the seas
each returning to earth itself
where no regard is found
for sights or sounds, thought or feeling
the multitude, unique cosmos perceived
dissipate into time past

Already it is happening even as we live
as our minds still see
and we still think and feel
The moments ever compounding,
already fade and fall away
The small sights we barely notice
as passing strangers in a busy terminal

iii.

Aside

This cake is baked
with regrets
and the dust of days.
I baked it myself.
I baked it from scratch,
and you know how hard it is
to find good scratch these days.
That's right.

I put it in a box
and put the box on a closet shelf
to be forgotten
mostly
except when it has to be moved aside
to find a scarf, or an old hat,
and I see it is still there
dried to a hard lump

iv.

Once happens, over and over and over again

When perspective wavers
When making do is all
Where ignorance is held to be revered
Simply because it is aged ignorance

Then the voices of the sky people
tell them what they want to hear
That they can think and say and do
                    horrible, horrific things
and still they are wonderful children

While they mold their golden calves
sell their birthright
for a bowl of porridge
sprinkled with the raisins of their
                    resentments

Aggrieved and deceived
wannabe goose-steppers, polyester

                              brownshirts

bullies, weasels and hollow brutes
bearing proudly the fruits of their lacking

over and over the lessons learned
paid in pain
the lessons are lost
denied, diminished, demurred

Memory is short
What new monsters await?
What new monsters
are being born, cooing

V.

Real men write poetry

I know the words by the sense of them
as a second language.
It seems I had no first.
I have to work them slowly,
read them over and over
hammering out their intent
peening the edges of implication

First found like fire or a sharp stone
approximations of the noticed world
In words were packed our understanding
Hard gained, mailable, tactile treasure
sustenance, shelter, soothe or sword
to share our wonder at this world
to explain it to ourselves

From before memory
the fellow travelers and the forgotten
the multitude of voices
they who have made the words sing,
placed them before us
Shaping lyric the real of experience
shining light in our space

Still worth the work
imperative we undertake
Turn them over, disassemble the mechanism
study the pieces scattered on the table
Put them back together, construe their
                                    operation
the interaction of the parts
the intent of the function

As a labor of life, a matter of necessity
Forging comprehension into syntax
Satisfaction in a job worth doing

as plowing a field or planing a board,
tasks of hands and backs and mind and sweat
making real in our moment
to grow and to shape where our paths will go

An inheritance to be handled
with thoughtful care, respecting the potency
knowing the transience too
and knowing this, facing it fully aware
with resolve to carry on regardless

Finding the human in the swerve of Lucretius,
drawing on the earthy heartbeat of Burns
Riding through the dark visions of Crane
(who I saw pass as I crouched in the desert)
To rue with him, to devise with them all,
shadows dropping a breadcrumb trail
across the oceans of time

vi.

As if, for example

A poem has its own mass
therein the effect of gravity
Flowing ideational
down over iamb stones
as a mountain stream
captured by the banks
yet creating its own form

Or as if hobbing a gear
Two axes of rotation, one at an angle
with infeed, perhaps even cross-feed
The flash of the turning brass
 bathed in cutting oil, the once-organic sap
The rumbling whirr of the drivers
Mathematics, Mechanics and Art

A moving sculpture taking form,
spinning hypnotically
Full depth, dwell, and done.
Another part ready to do work

So too another thought-artifact
impressed on paper, is set adrift into the ether
with small hopes to be carried on
in time to emerge, to engage a receptor
a meshing cog of form and fit
there touching a thing familiar
and turned in the mind, be useful

vii.

Hey!

I've looked around.
Peered into the cosmic vastness
and into clods of soil and sod

Into sand sifting between my fingers
At leaf and web and feather and shell,
the iridescence of fishes' scales

Clouds on the horizon
Lightning in the night sky
I've looked into faces and eyes, animal and other

Seen insects scrambling to get out of the way
Stood in the forest six feet from a deer
and watched as it walked carefully away

Long ago I played beneath the table
with my blocks and trucks, while above
the grownups, laughing, told their tales

(I wish I had been paying more
                        attention then)

I've listened to waves lapping for hours
drifting away, unconscious of the time
measured only from warmth to chill

At the edge of a canyon
I have felt the pull of its depth
and at the top of a mountain
I have watched the clouds pass below

I have looked around in this world
let it look through my eyes
feel through my being
each of us seeing

I've looked around
Looked and listened and thought and felt
This is the why
if any

viii.

Stage Fright
(When It Will Be My Turn To Be The Yorick)

Then were cinnamon girls and amber ladies
and ebony eyes, ethereal
Music was the air
Stones echoed overhead through the quad
snow wafted off the frozen lake
In laughter the clouds of our own breath
                          went before us

The days that would not end
They did
but carried on within
Day by day ticked away
All was potential then, become the actual now
the parting impossible to foretell

The path was trod, clocks were punched
Babies cried and children laughed and grew
Sun rose and set and we stood out in the night
with reverence for the twinkling stars
Feeling the earth revolving beneath our feet
Feeling our breath breathe into the universe

In the distance someone plays a tune
I recognize and smile
Someday, I like to think, perhaps, some guy,
                                        curious
like I would be, will lift my empty skull
like a shell to his ear and hear, not an ocean,
but an echoing guitar aching the Blues

ix.

Been There, Again

Here I sit while another evening wastes away
as if the days are infinite
The number may be unknown
But it is not then made innumerable

Each passing year smaller in proportion
circling faster and faster as its orbit
draws closer and closer to the center
vibrating a hum of melancholy gladness

We find ourselves living in the same time
but as in different dimensions
For some it is spring and life is bursting forth
some are in the fullness of their summers
with days that are long and warm

Others of us see the leaves turning,
the trees growing bare and cold winds
blow down the collars of our coats
as the sun rises lower and the days grow shorter
our mornings bring frost to the doorstep

In the future we will share the past
we make our beds, the rest will come

X.

Reprieve for the Homme de Porlock
of Lines Lost

Let me here confess
Sometimes the lines were written down
later to be found
stuck in book or drawer
Then comes an illumination...

Not all that is lost is precious.

Just part of the process
of arriving in the present

In time will be the tell

unable again to sleep

I wander down the hardwood hall,

trip in the dark over consequential

                              Inconsequentials,

stub my toe on an Almost,

and dancing on one foot

drive the upturned edge of a Never Was

into my bare sole.

The Difference Was Not
(For A Poet)

I saw your words
— wow — Raw dull angst
In a cold damp spring
a honeymoon of dust

All those people
present then, long ago
and we, living, so long ago
distant then and now, so far

So real in each moment
in the next turned to shadow
while memory's shards sear
Present of past unrealized

Here decays from the inside
the gut clenches
while birds full of color
snatch seeds from our patios

What is unseen
quietly and away they all fall
like words fall, in the forest
could we have spoken

Mooses Go Walking While Universe Unmoved Remains In Motion

For all who have been and all that will be
When time slides behind transparency
Don't look for them Up There, they will be all around

In every sunbeam, on every breeze
Don't look for them Up There, they will be all around
With all who have been and all that will be

On a frosty mist in the light of the moon
Where time slides behind transparency
Don't look for them Up There, they will be all around

Still hold to the memories that spring into mind
As time slides beyond this sight and sound
With all who have been and all that will be

In ripples on water or shadow of cloud
For all who have been and all that will be
Don't look for them Up There, they will be all around

While holding the memories that flow into mind
They dissolve into ether with nothing to bind
so don't look for me Up There, I will be gone

                                    but all around
With all who have been and in all that will be

The Bug
(There is Something Larger Than Us)

The insect looks up.

The form blots out the sky.

Is this god?

The last thing the insect hears

is his own crunching.

The Bird

Rounding the tree I emerge
from the woods, the path
opens back to the yard
and of a sudden I am met by a bird
A large crow, there in my track
In my yard, shining black, black eyes

He turns to regard my intrusion,
flexes his wings, steps deliberately,
moving tangentially to keep me in view
we each watch the other
only I am paused with unease

A bird sees things differently
A bird knows his needs
He knows his purpose, he is focused

we eye each other warily

He has slight concern with me

I am at most a peripheral distraction

He knows I am slow

He can quickly away

and I cannot follow him into the sky

The Bell

The bell can ring, ring, ring
but the rings quickly fade.
The bell seems substantial
but the difference is just density
and a slightly longer moment.
And for the world that holds the bell
yet only a slightly longer moment.

This day in which the bell rings,
these sounds, this sky,
the breeze that moves the grasses,
can never repeat, never be the same.
Moment after moment all fades,
moves and re-forms.
As vapor we walk among the illusions.

About the Leaves

where leaves
on the tree
high
high above
cling
unaware
of their
clinging

When one
beside
in one moment
drops
away
are they watching it
moving
strangely

on the air
drifting
falling
slowly
down
until landing
far
below ?

NO.
 They are leaves.

But what would
leaves think, feel
 - if they could -
still clinging
in the breeze
in the sun
watching ?

And
what then
when
in but a moment
there
falls
another ?

would we have
the inexplicable
wonder of it
expressed in chlorophyl
in shades of yellow
orange
and red,
glowing leafly
glory ?

Of Dwelling in Time

From here where I have come to dwell
 — Like a leaf carried on a steam catches
    on a fallen twig along the banks —
I stand looking up, beneath the misty
floating ghost of the surface once high above
of mountains that once were in this spot
pushed aside by glaciers
whose own surface then was a mile above
where I now dwell
here below the ghosts of the creatures
that wander high up in the air
and where at night
the fires of the passing hunters
still glow between earth and sky
Here I am deposited on this present surface
of rolling hills of southern till,

once sea bottom, then plains, then forest,
then slashed away
for farms of hard abundance
lost to economies of expedience,
returning to woods cut back again
to make this spot of my dwelling
where little streams flow from the hills
and mingling grow to meet
where waves wash into shores
and flow back again to sea
over and over and over
the sound of the eons

The Same As Any Star

When I think about it I realize
I have known you almost
as long as I have known anything.
Trying to shift myself in the crowd
to keep you in view,
awestruck at that astonishing girl
shining celestial on this dimming world.

Long dark hair, shining dark eyes,
a soft sweetness in the smile …
Beauty and presence so far above the real,
beyond possibility.
All around faded at the form of you.
We were four years old.
What, how, can you know at four?

Growing up as friends in a circle of friends
each knew the other well.

And while I knew, our friends knew,
the whole town knew,
anyone who saw us knew,
still you took your time.

When it finally came to be
it is hard to mark the moment.
It just was, it had always been so,
fully natural, no difference,
but for waking in a world
moment by moment, all new.

So, you with your one life,
the same as any star,
this lifetime later
and I, amazed still
you choose to walk with me.

The Hill

(I Saw Her Eyes Were Hazel)

Most of the morning we had climbed the hill.
Our packs were light.
Carry what you need, no more.
The forested side mostly shade and cool.

Through tunnels of limb and leaf
the path tried to disguise its goal
until near the top it gave out into a rolling meadow
sloping away down the other side.

In the cloud-sun now we ran out into the
                                   waist deep grasses
until you tumbled laughing, and I beside.
We lay there a long while, and looking at the sky
wondered at a blue so violet and gray.

From our bed of grass we looked out over

                              the valley below.

A small town lay sheltered in the green

                              hazy distance,

and as the sun began to lower to the hill behind us

we considered, ought we turn back or go ahead.

A small brook began just below where we were sitting,

and since all brooks lead somewhere,

holding hands, with the sun on our backs

we followed it into the valley.

And So

And we got married
making between us $4 an hour
putting it together
and the work was hard
and we did it
and we learned
and we had three children
yes, we knew and we did it
and we worked harder
and we played
eating lots of 'Soup Again'
and macaroni and grilled cheese
and those taste good
with laughter 'round the table
and the children grew

and the children learned
and the life filled it in
as we went along
and it wasn't always much
and it wasn't a fairytale
but it was a story
and we wrote it
and it wasn't always everything
but more than could be wished

The Friend

(A Fable)

I remembered her first name, not her last

So you reminded me

Back in the days her words were kaleidoscope

Colliding colors and thoughts

Sharp as broken glass

The souls of old friends

dangled from her rearview mirror

in feathers and beads

Incandescent blur seeking her Dharma

trying in vain to hide herself in motion

She tore lines down her highway

always moving away, leaves scattering in her path

receding from view

Impressed within the memories

So now, how many years later,

to crash into her, literally, entering a shop

That awkward moment when recognition dawns

looking into each other's eyes

Her eyes back and forth between us

then past us to some distant place

where she wished that she could be

eyes somehow frantic and concealing

"Hi! How are you? How have you been?" we offer.

   "Fine. Fine." Her eyes peering at each, quick,

                                 then again away.

"How is ... "

   "He left ten years ago. I've no idea."

"Are you back in town?"

   "Just a quick visit. My uncle died. "

"We're so sorry to hear that."

   "Yes, well. Isn't time a great thing?

                       All of my friends are dead."

Awkward pause. We glance at each other.
    "I'm sorry, I have to go. I'm late. I have to..."
"Of course," we say. "It's so nice to see you."
                                "We'll have to..."
    "Yes. Of course. That would be nice. Goodbye."
"Bye." "Bye."

We squeeze each other's arms, still intertwined,
watch as she walks – hurries – away
the back of her long coat, her scarf falling down,
her knit hat, purse and bags.
She leaves a trail of footprints
in the light snow on the sidewalk,
moving, as always, away from us

And as we turn to go our way it comes to me
Dharma is hard if you are chasing it while running away.
And I feel an appreciation for those uncertain days
and those long-faded friends

For her too, if I could share that
All of it and all of them, all those past moments
together came to be this day
so much recalled into memory
as the snowfall closes behind
receding once more from view

Today I can be grateful for this
                              moment taken,
sitting in my Adirondack chair
                              in the rain.
Grateful for my cap, and a beer in hand,
watching the wood fill with mist,
listening to the raindrops slap the leaves,
                              glistening silver.
Below, the small stream tumbles its stories
in words of liquid whispers.

The rain stops, and at some unseen cue
the birds, ever urgent,
seize the respite and return.

This evening, looking at my hands,
how they open and close at my mere wishing...
useful tools, servants to my bidding,
bringing to me my needs,
lifting cool drink, or food to my mouth,
shading my eyes to gaze the distance.

Turning a page or pushing my pen,
steadying me when unsure,
feeling my way in the dark.
Informing me of flame or ice,
sand and shell, leaf or stone...
or a woman's form.

On a lathe, turning the wheels, flying to the levers
to engage exactly at the precise moment
the tool point to pick up a thread...
An astonishing thing!

Hand over hand they have pulled me through life,
lacerated and stitched, scar over scar,
cut, hammered, sprains and cracked bones,
always there for more.

Hands like these once formed axes and bowls,
with sticks furrowed the soil,
wove garments and tapestries, and fought,
always fighting... yet carried hope forward

                                       like a bundle.

carved monuments, built civilizations,
etched their stories on walls or scrolls
to those who would follow, who could not be known.
Then they were passed, their labors into dust
with the daylight dreams which shaped
matter into meaning.

This evening, looking at my hands,
how they open and close at my mere wishing...
But to think, to know,
 not for always
That in time certain these too will lie rigid,
still, unminding of tasks left undone.

Of Seeds

I have spent some time in gardens,
real gardens with imaginary toads,
salamanders, snakes and bugs . . .
They hop, crawl, shine and slither at the periphery.
When you turn to look, they are not there.
Or sometimes they are there, so near to your hand
the hair stands on the back of your neck.
Then settles the real.

Real toads, real sun, real fingers in the real dirt.
Real smile in the real sweat of this real day.
The real, always there, in front of,
blocking and blinding the shimmering
which lies behind, that moves through us
on rivers of time.

So, my little seed, my scattering, curious spark,
come play here, child, where I can see you,
between these rows of lettuce and cucumbers.
Only take care for the vines.
You, digging your holes and piling the pebbles,
while I sit and warm in the sun like an old reptile.
You, intent in your task,
me, with my knife cleaning this carrot
which we will share.

Someday, perhaps, on a warm day, in a garden,
on a breeze,
this day will come back to you
and you will remember,
"I love you more than mosquito bites."

("Daddy! You don't love mosquito bites!")

To have reached this age of passing hours,
great fortune for the dim warm yellow
of my inefficient incandescent bulb
glowing the oak woodwork around me.

Glowing with reverence for those trees,
once living things, where now
the lines of the grains in these boards
each tell of seasons and growth, long ago.

Filling life yet with a sense of constancy
and subtle shades, notes and harmonies of light.
Hard strength beside the texture of this page,
these great and small gifts, how rich made the life.

Now, Roses

Late into an evening on a day when a song
had been stuck in my head
the tune bringing images of places long past
Recalling passages submerged in my mind
in hazy fragments, the feelings and friends
I pushed back my chair to shut down the device
but then on a whim I keyed in a name
Scanned down the page until there at the end
My heart stopped at – obit –

It can't be the same I held out as it opened
But then a face, and though older, the smile
                                    left no doubt
The spark in the eyes drew just the same
the years had dimmed neither
Now time did a stop, a choke rose in my throat

the world suddenly grayer, suddenly cold
stunned how the time had gone passed unnoticed
over a year and a half now while I never knew
of your life or location since decades ago

It's long since the times you would burst
                                    into my room
your newest-found album stuffed under your arm
the conversation started before you arrived
To show what you'd written and a bottle of wine
cynic and smart, intelligence sparking,
                                    humor that bit
a mind ever bounding, hard to keep up,
                        I was glad just to try
A sort-of older brother who for me opened views
that may not have been found except for
                                    through you.
Then you vanished in the west with a call
                        that was missed

And in between as the years fell away
I knew you were out there, in this world
                                    sharing time
There was comfort from that, a reassuring hope
I still always pictured that one day yet to come
I'd walk up to your house and knock on your door
with a bouquet of dead flowers and some
                                    cheap apple wine
To tell what we've wondered, to ask what
                                    we've done
To hear what music had carried us each through
                                    our years
and finally say what those moments had meant

But now I shall have to put that away too

So now I read of your life, your profession,

                                                                  your wife

children there also, the gloss of description

                                                we'll be lucky to get

that really tells nothing of the moments and days

The thoughts and the laughter, the rising

                                                each morning

to move on in the world to craft our own meaning

All that was missed in distance and time,

                                              what could have been shared

While the sorrow is now, the loss was for years

                                              and one day at a time

Dead flowers, old friend, for I must remain

Still glad for lives crossing that brief long ago

The Fade

We will live as long
as there are those who remember us,
who hear our voice.
When they are gone,
we are gone.
So many have fallen from memory,
into vapor, atoms dispersed . . .

While I remain able
I do what I can
to keep them with me, alive.
They who peopled the world,
my world, that world which we inhabited,
one by one left along the way.
Those great Aunts and Uncles, Grandparents,
                        and the many friends. . .

as I knew them, smiling, vital, working, laughing.
I keep the sun still on their faces.

So also in time will it be for Man.
Will the random winds remember, one day?
Will the ocean,
its waves consumed against some beach?
Will there be only bones to tell
until finally they too are gone?
The lucky ones will turn to stone.

"It's all over now, it's all in the past."

The words came out of the blue.
Surprise, so long the silence.
It must have surprised him too,
to be aloud.
He glanced at us, realizing we were there,
hearing, then turned back inward to himself.
No more to say, not meant to share.

The room is clinical, clean, the brightness dimmed.
We sit to the side, unsure in the waiting.
He is ninety-one and fell on the ice in his drive.
Five weeks later here we are, wondering...
Should we have, at some point,
decided something differently?
We are no longer young either,
the weight of mortality rides on our shoulders
where we once carried our children.

It sits, we sit, uncomfortably, waiting...

watching.

7

This is our Dad, we sitting here now, and he
reaching out in the air for phantoms of the mind.
What is there, in that space?

Is it some time-traveler from a black and white
Depression-era childhood... Mother? Father?
Uncle? School chum? A loved dog?
Is he dashing across the fresh-plowed farm field,
called for supper? Does the rain start to fall?

Is he lying in his bunk, crammed in below deck,
farther from home than he had ever been,
hardly more than a kid, among all those strangers,
feeling lost, wondering what the future

holds in wait?

Is he maybe, later on, piloting along his invisible path
through the clouds?
Breaking out into the sunlight above,
he wraps it back around.
He is one with the machine, tuned to the hum,
feeling, literally, with the seat of his pants.
It is here he where he finds his happiness, his peace.
Ceiling and visibility unlimited.

Or is it Mom? Is she young again, and so pretty,
as the girl he met? Does she smile at him like
in the pictures,
when they were so young, full of hope for life?
Or is it she, only a moment later, wife and mother,
ever energetic
competent and complete, partner, friend
and love ?
Yes, let it be like those,
before the age and suffering and decline.

What would they say to him, and he to them?
Do they only mouth their words,
which he strains his mind to hear?
Do they seek to comfort, to reassure?
I hope so, or just leave him be.

>

The moment arrives in stealth, all quiet.
No sound, no glow, no shadow, no feel.
We hold our own breath and wait ... watch ...

                                        wait ...

Then know.

In that moment, no magic, yet mystifyingly real
the peculiar wonder, the strange sense of it.
Is ... Is not.
Once passed, no word, no returning,
when we step from these dimensions
into timelessness.

The curator

Among these boxes I sit
The parents' house is emptied
Debris falls on me
Boxes too from when they had
emptied their own parents' houses
My life is curator
With my cup of coffee
I sit and I sort
Old photographs and brittle papers,
Little saved mementos, without their stories
The sunlight outside
glazes my open window frame
while the breeze carries in the scent
of a coming rain
These pictures I hold, my grandmother
a little girl on her grandparents' lap
and then they with their horses, their dogs
all loved, all long long gone

There too are small objects mixed in
Saltshakers and a cast iron cat
A blue bottle and a porcelain pitcher
These all held memories
Some I had heard, if only now a hazy murmur
The decorations of the homes
where I played as a child
I have to look away for a moment
and let myself breathe
The clock on the wall ticks
In my chest I can feel the time passing
A draft from the window
rustles the papers
I hear the rain begin to fall
I turn another picture, my grandparents
I see the smiles, I hear their laughter
From where I sit here now
I know what they did not

But the sun shined on them that day
and the breeze met their faces.
It was not black and white
It was as real as this

In Subtle Shades

Lasting love
lights life
in subtle shades

Not in brilliance
of blinding white
blank and sterile

Nor in dark
of blackest black
cold and void

Those each unperceiving
Look away or look nowhere
Seeing nothing

Love is in rose pink
under the wing
of a bird

In flowering petals
yellow, red, blue
dripping dew

In the soft calls
in the misty wood
green with leaf and moss

When golden sun
in pure blue sky
breaks the cobalt clouds

And sunrise and sunset
flare in orange and red
and promise renews

In rain drops
shining translucent
then singing to the seas

It flows on melodies
intertwining, apart
then together again

In a thousand glances
sparkling hazel
tells all that is true

Love lasts while
we live it
in colors and song

From flash to ash
an instant of being.
We burst into the light,
to the warmth.
Like quarks we pop into view, then vanish,
mass and energy dissipated
back into the stardust mash.

From the deep, dark and dreamless,
before self, before time,
into being, without intent.
So is the moment here.
I walk in the sunlight
within the drifting, churning cosmos,
holding tight to the minute things
to ease the vertigo.

Someday this shadow will cease to be
when indifferent nature is done with me.
But while I live to haunt this space
I pace.
Window to window comparing the views,
sentinel, seeking who knows?
In being, I roam.
Until I go to where time goes
I keep my ghost to the grindstone.

we, drawn here too
by chance
on this beach
timeless, everchanging

Quiet now and warm
cool waves lapping
Sand and smooth pebbles
Gulls circle, we pause

Here a fish
of bone and scales
half-rising in the sand
eyeless, gaping mouth

And there just aside
a gull too
bones, and feathers
still moving in the breeze

This fish once
slipped though these waters
swept with the flows
In glimmering sunlight

This gull drifted above
rode the air, sun
warming wings, intent
for the motions below

Here by the same chance
each come to apparent rest
in this moment
which also will not last

So here, now, we and they
in our moments, sun and sound,
wind and waves, to rearrange
with the next storm

In every moment,

moment by moment

everything changes always

Even eternity

becomes something else